HAIKUS OF
ALL SEASONS V

THE HEAVENS
AND THE EARTH

MAYUMI ITOH

In memory of

Miyazawa Kenji (1896–1933)

Contents

Note for paperback edition: This book is for on-demand printing. The actual page numbers (and page breaks and other formatting matters) may differ from the page numbers shown in the Table of Contents above, due to the formatting by Amazon that is used on the day of the book order.

List of photographs

Sources for all photographs are credited below except for those that were taken by the author.

Photograph 1. Itsukushima Shrine Torii, under Wikimedia Commons license, "Itsukushima Gate," January 4, 2013, https://upload.wikimedia.org/wikipedia/commons/thumb/0/0e/Itsukushima_Gate.jpg/1024px-Itsukushima_Gate.jpg

Photograph 2. Snowflakes, under Wikimedia Commons license, "Snowflakes on Windshield," December 15, 2013, https://commons.wikimedia.org/wiki/File:SnowflakesOnWindshield.JPG

Photograph 3. Mitsumata, under Wikimedia Commons license, "Edgeworthia chrysantha," April 6, 2014,

Photograph 7. Sea of clouds at Takeda Castle, under

Wikimedia Commons license, "Takeda Castle," December

5, 2010, https://commons.wikimedia.org/wiki/File:Flickr_-

bullets95-_DSC01859.jpg

Photograph 8. Mt. Yari, under Wikimedia Commons

license, "Mt. Yari from the ridge," August 15, 2013,

https://commons.wikimedia.org/wiki/File:北穂東稜から見

た槍ヶ岳_2013-08-15_-_Monto_Jari_de_la_monteĝo_-

_Mt._Yari_from_the_rigde_-_panoramio.jpg

Photograph 9. Porcelain art pair created by Meg Itoh after

the nursery rhyme, Hey Diddle Diddle, the Cow Jumped

over the Moon, taken by the author

Photograph 10. Hanging persimmons, under Wikimedia

Commons license, "Barn of Kanzo yashiki," November 12,

2010,

https://upload.wikimedia.org/wikipedia/commons/7/72/Kan

zo-yashiki-umaya.JPG

Photograph 11. Dwarf periwinkle after the sleet, taken by

the author

Photograph 12. Shirakawa-gō, under Creative Commons

license, "Ogimachi, Shirakawa, Ono District, Gifu

Prefecture," December 6, 2014,

https://commons.wikimedia.org/wiki/File:Ogimachi,_Shira

kawa,_Ono_District,_Gifu_Prefecture_501-5627,_Japan_-

panoramio(21).jpg

This book presents each haiku in both Japanese and English so that non-Japanese-speaking readers can fully appreciate it. The first page for a given haiku (on the left side) shows the original haiku in Japanese, which is made up of a combination of Chinese characters (*kanji*) and Japanese phonetic characters (*hiragana* and *katakana*). In accordance with the customs for writing haiku, the old spellings of *hiragana* are used for the original haiku.

Then, in order to facilitate a better understanding, especially for those who are studying Japanese, the original haiku is shown in a modern spelling in *hiragana* and *katakana*. This allows readers to see how the haiku is exactly pronounced phonetically. There are many ways to pronounce specific *kanji* words, and the original Japanese haiku does not indicate how each *kanji* word is actually pronounced. It is sometimes difficult even for Japanese readers to know the pronunciation. Therefore, the simpler rendition of each haiku only in modern *hiragana* and *katakana* will help.

Afterward, the identification of the season word for the haiku is given and some explanations of the cultural and historical backgrounds are added where applicable.

On the second page for a given haiku (on the right side), a romanization of the original Japanese haiku is provided, first, so that English-speaking readers can understand how the haiku is pronounced. The words in Roman letters are divided into smaller groups of syllables, for easier reading.

Then, an English translation of the haiku is presented. It is a paraphrasing of the haiku, rather than a literal translation, in order for it to make the best sense in English. Accordingly, for many cases, the word order of

the haiku might be different from the original haiku in
Japanese. It is followed by the English translations of the
season word and the explanations of the cultural and
historical backgrounds. This completes the presentation of
a given haiku.

All translations, including those of haikus, were
made by the author. For romanizing Japanese words, the
Hepburn style is primarily used, with macrons. However,
macrons are not used for words known in English without
macrons, as for Kyoto and Tokyo. Another exception is
that "n" is not converted to "m" for words where it
precedes "b, m, and p." Examples include tonbo, instead of
tombo; Gunma prefecture, instead of Gumma prefecture;
and tanpopo, instead of tampopo.

Names of Japanese persons are given with the
surname first, except for those who use the reversed order
in English. Honorific prefixes, such as doctor and mister,
are not used in the text, except in direct quotations.

Acknowledgments

I would like to thank all the members of *Hoshi no shima kukai* (the Haiku Society of Star Island, a new name for the Haiku Society of New York), past and present—including but not limited to Esaka Kinuyo, Hara Yasuko, Sakuhara Aya, and Tsukino Popona—as well as Tsuneo Akaha, Kent Calder, Toshiko Calder, Steve Clemons, Akiko Collcutt, Gerald Curtis, Joshua Fogel, Hoshi Hiroshi, Ronald Hrebenar, Ken Kawata, Donald Keene, Ellis Krauss, Mike Mochizuki, T. J. Pempel, Stephen Roddy, Gilbert Rozman, Richard Samuels, Vicki Wong, Donald Zagoria, and Quansheng Zhao, for continuous encouragement and inspirations. I extend my deep appreciation to Gregory Rewoldt and Meg Itoh for generous support.

Preface

This is the fifth haiku anthology by this author and

embraces three of the seven major themes of haiku: 1) the

seasons and the weather; 2) astronomy or the heavens; and

3) geography or the earth. As background information, this

book introduces anecdotes about the culture and history of

each subject, where applicable. For rules about haiku

making, please see *Haikus of All Seasons I: The Heavens

and The Earth* (2018).

This book is dedicated to the poet/writer Miyazawa

Kenji (August 1896–September 1933), whose works are

marked by an expansive and profound interest in the earth,

the heavens, the humanities, and religion, and many of the

haikus in this collection feature his life and works. Some

of the memorable works of Miyazawa are: *Ame nimo*

makezu (Strong in the Rain, 1934), *Ginga testudō no yoru*

(The Night of the Milky Way Railroad, 1934) *Kaze no*

Matasaburō (Matasaburō the Wind, 1934), and *Sero-hiki*

no Gōshu (Gauche, The Cellist, 1934).

85th anniversary memorial day of Miyazawa Kenji

September 21, 2018

January

Photograph 1. Itsukushima Shrine Torii, under Wikimedia Commons license, "Itsukushima Gate," January 4, 2013, https://upload.wikimedia.org/wikipedia/commons/thumb/0/0e/Itsukushima_Gate.jpg/1024px-Itsukushima_Gate.jpg

初茜

　　富士の霊験

　　　　あらたかに

はつあかね

　　ふじのれいげん

　　　　あらたかに

季語　初茜（新年）

元日の朝の茜空。

Hatsu akane

Fuji no reigen

arataka ni

The dawn on new year's day

renews

the sacred spirit of Mt. Fuji

Season word: *hatsu akane* (the dawn on new year's day; new year)

初日の出

　　高千穂の神

　　　目覚めたり

はつひので

　　たかちほのかみ

　　　めざめたり

季語　初日の出（新年）

日本神話によると、宮崎県の高千穂神社には、皇祖神（天皇の祖先）とその配偶神が祀られているという。

Hatsu hinode

Takachiho no kami

mezame tari

The sunrise on new year's day

has awakened gods and goddesses

in Takachiho

Season word: *hatsu hinode* (the sunrise on new year's day;

signifies new year)

According to Japanese mythology, Takachiho Shrine in

Miyazaki prefecture enshrines ancestral gods and

goddesses of the Japanese imperial family.

伊勢神宮

　　朝の光に

　　　　淑気満つ

いせじんぐう

　　あさのひかりに

　　　　しゅくきみつ

季語　淑気（新年）

新年を迎え、伊勢神宮の境内に瑞祥（ずいしょう）の気が

満ちている様子。

Ise jingū

    asa no hikari ni

        shukuki mitsu

At Ise Grand Shrine

    the morning sunlight shines through

        the atmosphere of blessings on new year's day

Season word: *shukuki* (the atmosphere of blessings on new

year's day; new year)

Ise Grand Shrine in Ise, Mie prefecture, is dedicated to the

Sun Goddess Amaterasu and ranks highest among all the

Shinto shrines in Japan.

厳島

　　初凪に乗り

　　　　神渡る

いつくしま

　　はつなぎにのり

　　　　かみわたる

季語　初凪（新年）

広島県にある宮島の厳島神社の新年の風景。

Itsukushima

hatsu nagi ni nori

kami wataru

At Itsukushima Shrine

the gods are crossing the sea

riding on the calm of the sea on new year's day

Season word: *hatsu nagi* (the calm of the sea on new

year's day; new year)

Itsukushima Shrine, located on Itsukushima Island

(Miyajima) in Hiroshima prefecture, is best known for its

"floating" torii gate, attracting many foreign tourists.

初春や

　　お題目聴く

　　　　花巻の里

はつはるや

　　おだいもくきく

　　　　はなまきのさと

季語　初春（新年）

「花巻の里」は、宮沢賢治（1896年－1933年）の生地、岩
手県花巻市（生誕当時は里川口村、亡くなった時には花
巻町）のこと。賢治は、法華経に帰依していた。法華経で
は、念仏ではなくお題目を唱える。

Hatsu haru ya

o daimoku kiku

Hanamaki no sato

New Year's Day

the field in Hanamaki

is listening to the Buddhist mantra

Season word: *hatsu haru* (*lit.*, "new spring" refers to the

new year; new year)

Miyazawa Kenji (1896–1933) was born in current

Hanamaki, Iwate prefecture. He subscribed to the Hoke

school of Buddhism, which chants its own mantra of the

Buddhist sutra.

明石の塔

　　新たな年を

　　　　刻みたり

あかしのとう

　　あらたなとしを

　　　　きざみたり

季語　　新たな年（年新た、新年）

兵庫県明石市は、日本標準時子午線（東経135度線）の町。明石市天文科学館には、時計塔が日本標準時子午線の真上に建設され、日本標準時のランドマークとなっている。

Akashi no tō

   arata na toshi o

      kizami tari

The clock tower at Akashi

   is marking the time

      of the new year

Season word: *aratana toshi* (new year; new year)

Akashi, Hyōgo prefecture, is the location of the Japan
Standard Time Meridian, 135 degrees east longitude. It is 9
hours ahead of the Prime Meridian at Greenwich, England.

御降や

　　　万の蕾を

　　　　　起こしたり

おさがりや

　　　まんのつぼみを

　　　　　おこしたり

季語　御降（新年）

御降（おさがり）は、元日から三日の間に降る慈雨のこと。

特別の恵みのように感ずる。

O sagari ya

    man no tsubomi o

        okoshi tari

The rain on new year's day

    has woken up

        a hundred thousand buds

Season word: *o-sagari* (the rain on the first three days of the new year; new year)

O-sagari (*lit.*, "blessings that the gods send down to Earth") refers to the rain on the first three days of the new year, which is considered the blessing from Heaven.

元旦の

　　噴火に慄く

　　　　桜島

がんたんの

　　ふんかにおののく

　　　　さくらじま

季語　　元旦（新年）

鹿児島県の桜島では、1914年（大正3年）1月に始まった噴火が4月まで続き、甚大な被害をもたらした。「桜島・大正大噴火」と言われる。

Gantan no

    funka ni ononoku

        Sakura jima

The eruption on new year's day

    has terrified

        Sakura Island

Season word: *gantan* (new year's day; new year)

In January 1914, Sakura Island, the active volcano in

Kagoshima prefecture, had eruption, which continued for a

month. This is recorded as the Great Eruption of Taishō on

Sakura Island. Taishō refers to the period of the Imperial

reign of Emperor Taishō Yoshihito (1879–1926). Taishō

1–Taishō 15 correspond to 1912–1926.

新燃岳

　　新春のマグマ

　　　　噴き出づる

しんもえだけ

　　しんしゅんのマグマ

　　　　ふきいづる

季語　　新春（新年）

2011年1月、鹿児島県霧島市にある霧島山の新燃岳が
爆発的噴火した。

Shinmoe dake

    shin shun no maguma

        fuki izuru

At Mt. Shinmoe

    the magma of the new year

        has erupted

Season word: *shin shun* (new year; new year)

Mt. Shinmoe is part of the Mt. Kirishima Volcano Group,

in Kagoshima prefecture. In January 2011, a magma

eruption occurred there, the first such eruption in 300 years.

The volcanic activity has continued to this day.

若菜野や

　　　童と嫗

　　　　手を繋ぎ

わかなのや

　　わらべとおうな

　　　　てをつなぎ

季語　若菜野（新年）

若菜は、春の七草の総称で、七草粥に入れる菜のこと。その若菜を摘む所を若菜野という。

Wakana no ya

    warabe to ōna

       te o tsunagi

In the field of spring herbs

    the child and the grandmother

       are walking hand in hand

Season word: *wakana no* (field of spring herbs; new year)

Wakana refers to the seven specific spring herbs that are
mixed in rice porridge, which Japanese eat on the seventh
day of January, for good luck and longevity.

February

Photograph 2. Snowflakes, under Wikimedia Commons

license, "Snowflakes on Windshield," December 15, 2013,

https://commons.wikimedia.org/wiki/File:SnowflakesOnWi

ndshield.JPG

雪の花

　　　万の神の

　　　　　巫女となり

ゆきのはな

　　　よろずのかみの

　　　　　みことなり

季語　雪の花（雪の結晶、冬）

雪の花は、雪の結晶の雅語。どれ一つとして同じ形のない

千差万満な雪の結晶は、まさに、雪の神の創った花のよう

である。

Yuki no hana

    yorozu no kami no

        miko to nari

The snowflakes

    have become the maiden attendants

        for every god

Season word: *yuki no hana* (*lit.*, "snow flowers" refers to snowflakes; winter)

Every snowflake has a unique pattern of its own. None of them have the same pattern.

大氷麗

　　賢治の心

　　　　溶かしたり

おおつらら

　　けんじのこころ

　　　　とかしたり

季語　　氷麗（冬）

賢治は、宮沢賢治（1896年−1933年）のこと。東北の岩手県花巻市（生誕当時は里川口村、亡くなった時には花巻町）で生まれ育った。

Ō tsurara

Kenji no kokoro

tokashi tari

The enormous icicles

have melted

Kenji's heart

Season word: *tsurara* (icicles; winter)

Kenji refers to the poet/writer Miyazawa Kenji (1896–
1933), who was born in current Hanamaki, Iwate
prefecture, in the northeastern region of Japan.

アイス・サークル

　　生き物のごと

　　　　生まれたり

アイス・サークル

　　いきもののごと

　　　　うまれたり

季語　アイス・サークル（冬）

アイス・サークルとは、川の氷が輪を作るという奇妙な現象
のこと。

Aisu sākuru

   ikimono no goto

      umare tari

The ice circles

   have sprung up

      as if they were living things

Season word: *aisu sākuru* (ice circles; winter)

"Ice circles" refer to a curious phenomenon in which ice in
a river forms in the shape of a circle and floats on the river.

氷柱落つ

　　氷神様の

　　　　武者震ひ

つららおつ

　　うじがみさまの

　　　　むしゃぶるい

季語　氷柱(冬)

Tsurara otsu

ujigami sama no

musha burui

The icicle fell

and the local guardian god shivered

in a dignified fashion like a samurai

Season word: *tsurara* (icicle; winter)

除雪車の

　　作りし街の

　　　　樹氷の森

じょせつしゃの

　　つくりしまちの

　　　　じゅひょうのもり

季語　　樹氷（冬）

Josetsu sha no

tsukuri shi machi no

juhyō no mori

The woods of ice monster trees

in the city street

were made by the snow removal trucks

Season word: *juhyō* (*lit.*, "tree ice," tree covered with ice,

'ice monster'; winter)

The ice dumped and accumulated at the street side looks

like the wood of ice sculptures of 'ice monster' trees.

シベリアの

　　定期便なり

　　　　三寒四温

シベリアの

　　ていきびんなり

　　　　さんかんしおん

季語　三寒四温（冬）

Shiberia no

    teiki bin nari

        san kan shi on

Siberia

    sends regular winter airmail

        a "cycle of three cold and four warm days"

Season word: *sankan shion* (*lit.*, "three cold and four warm days"; winter)

The refers to the seven-day cycle of the Siberian high-pressure air mass carried to Japan, in which three cold days are followed by four warmer days.

雪解風

　　六の花びら

　　　　散らしたり

ゆきげかぜ

　　むつのはなびら

　　　　ちらしたり

季語　雪解風（春）　六の花（冬）

六の花（むつのはな）は、雪の結晶の別称。この句は、厳
密に言えば季重なりであるが、雪解風が主季語で、六の
花と齟齬がないので、許容される。

Yukige kaze

  mutsu no hana bira

    chirashi tari

The snow-melting wind

  is scattering

    the petals of snowflakes

Season word: *yukige kaze* (*lit.*, "snow-melting wind" refers

to the early spring wind; spring)

Mutsu no hana (*lit.*, "six-petalled flower") is a poetic

expression for snowflakes.

淡雪や

　　儚き命

　　　　紡ぐトシ

あわゆきや

　　はなかきいのち

　　　　つむぐトシ

季語　淡雪（消えやすい春の雪、春）

宮沢賢治（1896年－1933年）の最大の理解者であった

妹トシ（1898年－1922年）は、幼少時から成績優秀で、

日本女子大学卒業後、母校の花巻高等女学校の教師と

なるが、結核を患い、24歳の若さで夭逝した。

Awa yuki ya

hakanaki inochi

tsumugu Toshi

The ephemeral light spring snow

Toshi lived

an ephemeral life

Season word: *awa yuki* (light spring snow; spring)

Toshi (1898–1922) refers to Miyazawa Kenji's younger

sister. She was bright and supported his works. Toshi

graduated from the Japan Women's University and began

teaching at her alma mater, the Hanamaki Higher Women's

School, but then died of tuberculosis at age 24.

名残雪

　　別れの竹林

　　　　さざめきて

なごりゆき

　　わかれのちくりん

　　　　さざめきて

季語　名残雪（春）

Nagori yuki

    wakare no chiku rin

        sazameki te

The leaves of the bamboo grove

    make a sad rustling sound

        to say good-bye to the last snow

Season word: *nagori yuki* (*lit.*, "farewell snow" means the last snow of the season; spring)

雪流れ

　　破間川の

　　　　遊覧船

ゆきながれ

　　あぶるまがわの

　　　　ゆうらんせん

季語　　雪流れ（春）

新潟県魚沼市の破間（あぶるま）川では、雪解け水がダム湖に流れ込み、水位が上昇すると、湖面を覆う雪が割れて、あたかも流氷のように漂う。この現象のことを「雪流れ」という。

Yuki nagare

    Aburuma gawa no

        Yūran sen

The floating snow

    on the Aburuma River

        is moving like a sightseeing boat

Season word: *yuki nagare* (*lit.*, "floating snow"; spring)

Yuki nagare on a river is a natural phenomenon similar to the *ryūhyō* (floating ice) in the northern oceans, such as the Sea of Okhotsk, in the early spring. Aburuma River runs in Uonuma, Niigata prefecture.

March

Photograph 3. Mitsumata, under Wikimedia Commons license, "Edgeworthia chrysantha," April 6, 2014, "https://commons.wikimedia.org/wiki/File:Edgeworthia_ch rysantha_0256.jpg

春萌す

　　萌黄の風を

　　　　呼ぶ野原

はるきざす

　　もえぎのかぜを

　　　　よぶのはら

季語　春萌す（春）

Haru kizasu

moegi no kaze o

yobu nohara

The signs of spring

the field sends

for the pale green wind

Season word: *haru kizasu* (the early signs of spring;

spring)

雪解や

　　せせらぎの音

　　　　緩みたり

ゆきどけや

　　せせらぎのおと

　　　　ゆるみたり

季語　雪解（春）

Yuki doke ya

    seseragi no oto

        yurumi tari

The melting snow

    makes the sound of the river

        gentle and soft

Season word: *yuki doke* (melting snow; spring)

春一番

　　神宿る島の

　　　　空と海

はるいちばん

　　かみやどるしまの

　　　　そらとうみ

季語　　春一番（春）

福岡県宗像市の玄界灘にある孤島沖ノ島は、宗像大社の
神領で、沖津宮（おきつぐう）が鎮座し、「神宿る島」と呼ば
れる。2017年、この一帯は、「『神宿る島』宗像・沖ノ島と
関連遺産群」としてユネスコ世界遺産リストに登録された。

Haru ichiban

kami yadoru shima no

sora to umi

The first spring gust

is blowing on the sacred island of the gods

and into the sky and the sea

Season word: *haru ichiban* (first spring gust; spring)

Okinoshima Island in Munakata, Fukuoka prefecture, is the

location of Munakata Shrine and is called the "Sacred

Island." In 2017, the area was registered with UNESCO

World Heritage as the Sacred Island of Okinoshima and

Associated Sites in the Munakata Region.

渦潮や

　　鳴門の船頭

　　　　奮ひ立つ

うずしおや

　　なるとのせんどう

　　　　ふるいたつ

季語　　渦潮（春）

鳴門海峡にある渦潮の速度は日本で一番速く、「世界三大潮流」に数えられているほどである。干満の差が一年中で最も大きくなる春の彼岸の頃に、渦潮の速度が最大となるという。観光船は渦潮のすぐそばを通り、人気がある。

Uzushio ya

    Naruto no sendō

       furui tatsu

The giant whirlpool

    the boatman for Naruto sightseeing

       is thrilled

Season word: *uzushio* (whirlpool; spring)

Whirlpools become the fastest around the time of the

Spring Equinox. The whirlpools in Naruto Strait, located

between Naruto, Tokushima prefecture, and Awaji Island,

Hyōgo prefecture, are some of the fastest whirlpools in the

world, and sightseeing boats sail over the whirlpools.

水温む

　　清流の

　　　　青のきらめく

みずぬるむ

　　せいりゅうの

　　　　あおのきらめく

季語　　水温む（春）

清流に渓流植物が成長し始める様子が清々しい。

Mizu nurumu

seiryū no

ao kirameku

The water warms up

and the grasses in the clear stream

are shining

Season word: *mizu nurumu* (the water warms up; spring)

Rheophytes, aquatic plants that live in fast moving water,

begin to grow in the spring.

催花雨や

　　濡るゝ大地の

　　　　ときめきて

さいかうや

　　ぬるるだいちの

　　　　ときめきて

季語　催花雨（春）

Saika u ya

nururu daichi no

toki meki te

The spring rain that brings forth flowers

is moistening the earth

and making it excited

Season word: *saika u* (spring rain that induces plants to

flower; spring)

屋島の戦

　　春風に舞ふ

　　　扇かな

やしまのいくさ

　　はるかぜにまう

　　　おうぎかな

季語　　春風（春）

元暦（げんりゃく）2年2月19日（新暦1185年3月22日）、
源氏方の那須与一（1169？－1189？）が、屋島の戦い
で平家方の軍船の柱の頭部に掲げられた夕陽に光る扇
の的を射落としたという伝説。『源平盛衰記』に記される。

Yashima no ikusa

   haru kaze ni mau

      ōgi kana

At the Battle of Yashima

   the folding fan

      was flown in the spring wind

Season word: *haru kaze* (spring wind; summer)

The historical chronicle records that Nasu no Yoichi

(1169?–1189?) shot an arrow into the target bull's eye of a

folding fan hoisted on top of a mast on a military ship of

the Heike enemy during the Battle of Yashima in February

1185, the last stage of the Genpei War between the Genji

and the Heike. Descendants of Nasu still exist today.

春驟雨

　　一雨ごとの

　　　　緑かな

はるしゅうう

　　ひとさめごとの

　　　　みどりかな

季語　春驟雨（春）

春驟雨（はるしゅうう）は、春に降る、雨足の強いにわか雨
のこと。

Haru shūu

hito same goto no

midori kana

The spring rain shower

makes the earth green

every time

Season word: *haru shūu* (spring rain shower; spring)

山の里

　　結香の風

　　　　芳しく

やまのさと

　　むすびきのかぜ

　　　　かんばしく

季語　　結香(春)

結香(むすびき)は三椏の別名。ジンチョウゲ科の低木で
群生する。黄色の小花が甘い香りを放つ。

Yama no sato

   musubiki no kaze

     kanbashi ku

In the mountain village

   the wind of the Oriental paperbush

     sends out its fragrance

Season word: *musubiki* (Oriental paperbush; spring)

Musubiki is a poetic name for *mitsumata* (Oriental paperbush), which has fragrant dainty yellow flowers in the spring.

春雷や

　　雲仙岳を

　　　　鎮めたり

しゅんらいや

　　うんぜんだけを

　　　　しずめたり

季語　春雷（春）

長崎県にある雲仙岳は、1792年に大噴火し、約1万5千人の死者を出した。1990年の大噴火では、43名の死者を出したが、この噴火活動は1995年3月まで続いた。

Shun rai ya

    Unzen dake o

        shizume tari

The spring thunder and lightning

    has quelled

        Mt. Unzen

Season word: *shun rai* (spring thunder and lightning;

spring)

Mt. Unzen is part of an active volcano group in Nagasaki

prefecture in the Kyūshū region. The 1792 eruption killed

14,524 people. Another large eruption in 1990 killed 43

people, including three foreign volcanologists. This

volcanic activity continued until March 1995.

April

Photograph 4. Cherry blossoms covered with frozen snow, taken by the author

春と修羅

　　　若き詩人の

　　　　　光と影

はるとしゅら

　　　わかきしじんの

　　　　　ひかりとかげ

季語　　春（春）

宮沢賢治（1896年−1933年）の口語詩『心象スケッチ
春と修羅』（1924年）に寄せて。賢治は「おれはひとりの修
羅なのだ」と記している。妹トシの死を悼む「永訣の朝」、ト
シの魂との交流を求める「青森挽歌」などが収録される。

Haru to Shura

   wakaki shijin no

      hikari to kage

Spring and Asura

   the light and shadow

      of the young poet

Season word: *haru* (spring; spring)

Miyazawa Kenji (1896–1933) wrote an anthology of poems

entitled *Haru to Shura* ("An Asura in Spring"). Asura,

power-seeking deities with three heads and three faces and

six arms in Hinduism, became deities of belligerence in

Buddhism and one of the guardian gods of Buddha. Asura

could be interpreted as a demon in Kenji.

春霞

　　太古の杜の

　　　　息遣ひ

はるがすみ

　　たいこのもりの

　　　　いきづかい

季語　春霞（春）

Haru gasumi

taiko no mori no

iki zukai

The spring haze

the sacred wood of ancient times

is breathing quietly

Season word: *haru gasumi* (spring haze; spring)

麗らかに

　　光の精の

　　　　微睡みて

うららかに

　　ひかりのせいの

　　　　まどろみて

季語　麗らか（春）

Uraraka ni

hikari no sei no

madoromi te

In the gentle, beautiful spring

the fairy of light

is dozing

Season words: *uraraka* (gentle, beautiful spring; spring)

土香る

　　春の野に会ふ

　　　春の風

つちかおる

　　はるののにあう

　　　はるのかぜ

季語　春の野（春）　春の風（春）

Tsuchi kaoru

haru no no ni au

haru no kaze

The earth gives forth its scent

and the spring wind

meets the spring field

Season words: *haru no no* (spring field; spring) and *haru no kaze* (spring wind; spring)

草萌ゆる

　　パステルカラーの

　　　山と空

くさもゆる

　　パステルカラーの

　　　やまとそら

季語　　草萌ゆる（春）

Kusa moyuru

pasuteru karā no

yama to sora

The grasses burst into growth

and paint the mountain and the sky

in pastel colors

Season word: *kura moyuru* (grasses burst into growth;

spring)

青き踏む

　　命の讃歌

　　　高らかに

あおきふむ

　　いのちのさんか

　　　たからかに

季語　青き踏む（春）

青き踏む（踏青、とうせい）は、春の野で青々とした草を踏
みしめて歩くこと。

Aoki fumu

  inochi no sanka

    takaraka ni

Walking on the green grasses in the spring field

  which are singing

    the song of life cheerfully

Season word: *aoki fumu* (walking on the green grasses in

the spring field; spring)

春嵐

　　西之島

　　　　また揺り起こし

はるあらし

　　にしのしま

　　　　またゆりおこし

季語　春嵐（春）

小笠原諸島の無人島西之島は、1973年、海底火山活動により生じた火山島。2013年、近くの噴火により新島ができたが、その後、西之島と合体した。噴火活動は、2016年に一旦沈降したが、2017年4月、再び活発化した。

Haru arashi

    Nishi no shima

        mata yuri okoshi

The spring storm

    has shaken

        Nishi no shima again

Season word: *haru arashi* (spring storm; spring)

Nishi no shima, part of the Ogawawara Islands in the

Pacific Ocean (administratively belonging to Tokyo

prefecture), was born out of an undersea volcanic eruption

in 1973. The volcanic island has kept expanding due to the

continuous eruptions, with the latest being in April 2017.

花冷や

　　異人の眠る

　　　　五輪塔

はなびえや

　　いじんのねむる

　　　　ごりんとう

季語　　花冷（春）

異人は、三浦按針（ウィリアム・アダムイス、1564年−1620年）のこと。神奈川県横須賀市に按針と妻の、二基の五輪塔が建てられている。これは位のある人に用いられる宝筐印塔（ほうきょういんとう）という立派な様式の塔である。

Hana bie ya

    ijin no nemuru

        gorin tō

The cold day in the cherry blossom season

  embraces the five-layered memorial stele

    underneath which the soul of the foreigner rests in peace

Season word: *hana bie* (a cold day in the cherry blossom

season; spring)

The English navigator, William Adams (Japanese name,

Miura Anjin, 1564–1620), was given the title of samurai by

the Tokugawa shogunate government. A respectable

memorial stele was made for him at Jōdo Temple in current

Yokosuka, Kanagawa prefecture, which stands today.

温暖化

　　桜前線

　　　　北へ去る

おんだんか

　　さくらぜんせん

　　　　きたへさる

季語　桜前線（春）

桜の開花時期の早まりは、地球温暖化による気象変動の
一つである。

Ondan ka

    sakura zensen

        kita e saru

Global warming

    has made the "cherry blossom front"

        move to the north

Season word: *sakura zensen* ("cherry blossom front";

spring)

Like daily weather forecast of air fronts, Japanese have a

daily forecast of "cherry blossom fronts" in spring. These

days, the cherry blossom fronts have moved north faster.

真珠星

　　真白き乙女の

　　　　願い星

しんじゅぼし

　　ましろきおとめの

　　　　ねがいぼし

季語　　真珠星（スピカ、春）

春の夜空に白く輝く真珠星は、乙女座の一等星、スピカの

和名。スピカは、牛飼い座の一等星、アルクトゥルス（オレ

ンジ色）と北斗七星とともに「春の大曲線」を描く。

Shinju boshi

    mashiroki otome no

        negai boshi

The Pearl Star

    shines as if it were the wishing star

        of the pure white maiden

Season word: *shinju boshi* (*lit.*, "Pearl Star," Spica; spring)

Shinju boshi (Pearl Star) is the Japanese name for Spica,

the alpha star of the constellation Virgo.

May

Photograph 5. Spring meadow with buttercup blossoms,

taken by the author

風光る

　　日長を遊ぶ

　　　すがねかな

かぜひかる

　　ひながをあそぶ

　　　すがねかな

季語　風光る（春）

すがねは、スゲ（菅）の根のこと。ここから、長いことを意味
する枕詞となった。女子の名前にも使われる。

Kaze hikaru

   hinaga o asobu

      sugane kana

The wind shines

   the suge plant roots

      play in the daylong light

Season word: *kaze hikaru* (wind shines; spring)

Sugane refers to the roots of a slender grass plant called suge (carex); hence the word is used as an epithet ("pillow word") for something long, as in "a long spring day." It is also a girl's name.

信濃路や

　　記憶辿りて

　　　　山辛夷

しなのじや

　　きおくたどりて

　　　　やまこぶし

季語　山辛夷（春）

堀辰雄（1904年－1953年）の随筆集、『大和路・信濃路』
（1943年）の一編「辛夷の花」は、全国の中学の教科書に
掲載された。

Shinano ji ya

kioku tadori te

yama kobushi

On the Shinano Road

one is tracing the old memories

in search of the mountain magnolia

Season word: *yama kobushi* (kobushi magnolia; spring)

"Kobushi no haha" ("The kobushi magnolia," 1943), the

essay by Hori Tatsuo (1904–1953) about the Shinano Road

in Nagano prefecture, was included in middle-school

textbooks nationwide.

由蘖や

　　眠る大地の

　　　　蘇り

ゆうげつや

　　ねむるだいちの

　　　　よみがえり

季語　由蘖（春）

由蘖（ゆうげつ）とは、樹木の切り株や根元に生える若芽
のこと。

Yūgetsu ya

nemuru daichi no

yomigaeri

The new buds

have appeared on the old tree trunk

and the life of the earth has been renewed

Season word: *yūgetsu* (new tree buds; spring)

Yūgetsu refers to new tree buds growing on old tree trunks

or at the roots.

初虹や

　　野辺の地蔵に

　　　　花供へ

はつにじや

　　のべのじぞうに

　　　　はなそなえ

季語　初虹（春）

初虹は、春初めて立つ虹のこと。

Hatsu niji ya

    nobe no jizō ni

        hana sonae

The first spring rainbow

    is offering flowers

        to the jizō statue in the field

Season word: *hatsu niji* (first spring rainbow; spring)

A jizō statue refers to a stone statue of the guardian gods of unborn children and their mothers. Jizō stone statues are a ubiquitous presence in the countryside.

雛孵る

　　微睡む春を

　　　　起こしたり

ひなかえる

　　まどろむ

　　　　はるをおこしたり

季語　雛孵る（春）

Hina kaeru

madoromu haru o

okoshi tari

The chicks have hatched

and the dozing spring has awakened

with excitement

Season word: *hina kaeru* (chicks have hatched; spring)

山笑ふ

　　六甲の風よ

　　　海の風

やまわらう

　　ろっこうのかぜよ

　　　うみのかぜ

季語　山笑う（春）

六甲は、兵庫県神戸市の西北にある六甲山のこと。

Yama warau

Rokkō no kaze yo

umi no kaze

The wind from Mt. Rokkō meets

the wind from the sea

and the mountain smiles

Season word: *yama warau* (mountain smiles; spring)

Mt. Rokkō is located in Kobe, Hyōgo prefecture.

春浪や

　　白砂の松と

　　　　羽衣と

はるなみや

　　はくさのまつと

　　　　はごろもと

季語　春浪（春）

羽衣伝説に寄せて。

Haru nami ya

hakusa no matsu to

hagoromo to

The spring waves

the pine grove and the white feather gown

lay on the white beach

Season word: *haru nami* (spring waves; spring)

A Japanese legend called Hagoromo has it that heavenly

maidens wearing *hagoromo* (*lit.*, "feather robe," white veil-

like robes) descended to the earth and bathed in the water.

As a man hid the robe of one of the maidens, she could not

fly back to the heaven and married him. Years later he

returned the robe to her and she ascended to heaven.

紫宸殿

　　強者慕ぶ

　　　　花橘

ししんでん

　　つわものしのぶ

　　　　はなたちばな

季語　　花橘（夏）

橘自体は、実のことをさすので秋の季語となる。紫宸殿は
京都御所の内裏の中にある儀式を行うための正殿。前庭
には、左近の桜（東）と右近の橘（西）が植えられている。

Shishin den

    tsuwa mono shinobu

        hana tachibana

At Shishin Palace

    tachibana orange blossoms

        reminisce about the warriors of the past

Season word: *hana tachibana* (tachibana orange blossoms; summer) (tachibana itself is a fruit and signifies autumn) The Shishin Palace is the ceremony hall of the Inner Palace of the Imperial family in Kyoto. It is adorned with a cherry tree on the left (east side) and a tachibana orange tree on the right (west side), in front of which the two generals of the Inner Palace Guards used to stand.

山開き

　　頂きはるか

　　　雪の壁

やまびらき

　　いただきはるか

　　　ゆきのかべ

季語　　山開き（夏）

2018年5月16日、岐阜県北アルプス・乗鞍岳を通る山岳道路、乗鞍スカイラインが、冬季閉鎖を終えて全面開通した。5メートルの「雪の壁」に挟まれた道路をバスが運行。終点の畳平で、山開き祭があり、安全祈願が行われた。

Yama biraki

    itadaki haruka

       yuki no kabe

At the opening of the mountaineering season

    the "walls of snow"

       climb to the high summit of Mt. Norikura

Season word: *yama hiraki* (opening of the mountaineering

season; summer)

On May 16, 2018, the Norikura Skyline, a road that runs on

Mt. Norikura, in the Northern Japan Alps, was opened for

the season. Earlier, snow removal trucks had cleared the

road and tourist buses ran between the 16-foot high "walls

of snow," heading to the summit.

夏の宵

　　金星寝入り

　　　木星起きる

なつのよい

　　きんせいねいり

　　　もくせいおきる

季語　　夏の宵（夏）

2018年5月23日の宵の頃、金星が西の空に沈むと同時に、木星が東の空から上った。半月を過ぎた月はその二つの惑星の間に浮かんでいた。

Natsu no yoi

Kinsei neiri

Mokusei okiru

The summer evening

Venus is going to sleep

while Jupiter is waking up

Season word: *natsu no yoi* (summer evening; spring)

In the evening on May 23, 2018, Venus set in the west, while Jupiter rose in the east. The waxing half moon was in between the two planets.

June

Photograph 6. Double rainbow, under Wikimedia Commons license, "Double rainbows Kitaakita," October 9, 2016, https://commons.wikimedia.org/wiki/File:Double_rainbows _Kitaakita.jpg

梅雨しきり

　　農夫労はる

　　　　詩人をり

つゆしきり

　　のうふいたわる

　　　　しじんり

季語　　梅雨しきり（夏）

詩人は宮沢賢治（1896年−1933年）のこと。賢治の詩

「雨ニモマケズ」へのオマージュ。賢治の死後、手帳が発

見され、この詩が、1931年11月3日に記されていた。

Tsuyu shikiri

   nōfu itawaru

      shijin ori

At the peak of the rainy season

   the poet visits the farm

      and consoles the farmers

Season word: *tsuyu shikiri* (peak of the rainy season; summer)

This is a homage to the posthumously found poem, *Ame nimo makezu* (*lit.*, "undeterred by the rain") by Miyazawa Kenji (1896–1933), who had genuine compassion for farmers in his hometown, Hanamaki, Iwate prefecture.

二重虹

　　賢治の夢や

　　　果てしなく

ふたえにじ

　　けんじのゆめや

　　　はてしなく

季語　二重虹（夏）

賢治は、宮沢賢治（1896年－1933年）のこと。

Futae niji

Kenji no yume ya

hateshi naku

The double rainbow

the dream of Kenji

grows endlessly

Season word: *futae niji* (double rainbow; summer)

Kenji refers to Miyazawa Kenji (1896–1933), who had an expansive and profound interest in various subjects in the humanities, nature, astronomy, and other natural sciences.

梅雨曇

　　雨の音待つ

　　　　和傘かな

つゆぐもり

　　あめのおと

　　　　まつわがさかな

季語　梅雨曇（夏）

愛知県名古屋市にある徳川園では、毎年、花菖蒲の時期

になると、来園者に綺麗な美濃和紙を貼った和傘を貸し

出して、雨の中、花菖蒲園を散策できるようにしている。

Tsuyu gumori

ame no oto matsu

wagasa kana

On the cloudy day in the rainy season

the Japanese umbrellas are waiting

for the sound of the raindrops

Season word: *tsuyu gumori* (cloudy day during the rainy

season; summer)

Tokugawa Garden in Nagoya, Aichi prefecture, has a rental

service of traditional umbrellas, made of beautiful Mino

paper, so that visitor can enjoy viewing irises in the rain.

雲海や

　　阿蘇の夜明けを

　　　包み込み

うんかいや

　　あそのよあけを

　　　つつみこみ

季語　雲海（夏）

2018年6月、熊本県の阿蘇山の裾に雲海が現れ、夜明

けの町をすっぽりと包み込んだ。それは、あたかも町全体

が消えてしまったように見えた。

Unkai ya

    Aso no yoake o

      tsutsumi komi

The sea of clouds

    covered the town around Mt. Aso at dawn

      and made it disappear

Season word: *unkai* (sea of clouds; summer)

At dawn in June 2018, a dense mist appeared at the foot of volcanic Mt. Aso and covered the whole town, making the town disappear.

風薫る

　　皇女の神輿

　　　　伊勢路往く

かぜかおる

　　こうじょのみこし

　　　　いせじゆく

季語　　風薫る（夏）

この句の皇女は、天皇に代わって伊勢神宮に仕えた「斎
王」と呼ばれる皇族の女性のこと。十二単を纏った斎王の
京都から伊勢までの大行列のことを「斎王群行」と呼ぶ。

Kaze kaoru

   kōjo no mikoshi

      Ise ji yuku

In the fragrant wind

   the portable shrine carrying the Imperial princess

      proceeds on the Ise Road

Season word: *kaze kaoru* (fragrant wind; summer)

The "Imperial princess" refers to the 'Princess Saiō' who served at Ise Grand Shrine on behalf of emperors over generations during the Heian period. The procession of the princess to Ise Grand Shrine from Kyoto was grand.

青嵐

　　　松の記憶の

　　　　　久しかり

あおあらし

　　　まつのきおくの

　　　　　ひさしかり

季語　青嵐（夏）

Ao arashi

matsu no kioku no

hisashi kari

The wind blowing through green leaves

carries the memories of the pine tree

that go far back in time

Season word: *ao arashi* (*lit.*, "green storm," early summer

wind blowing through green leaves; summer)

皐月躑躅

　　白砂の庭に

　　　　打ち寄せて

さつきつつじ

　　はくさのにわに

　　　　うちよせて

季語　　皐月躑躅（サツキ・ツツジ、夏）

滋賀県甲賀市にある大池寺（だいちじ）の蓬莱庭園は、小
堀遠州（小堀政一、1579年−1647年）作の枯山水庭で、
剪定されたサツキ・ツツジ（波に見立てられる）と白砂の海
のコントラストが美しい。

Satsuki tsutsuji

hakusa no niwa ni

uchi yosete

The sea of white sand

is engulfed

by the waves of satsuki azaleas

Season word: *satsuki tsutsuji* (satsuki azaleas; summer)
Satsuki tsutsuji grows like a crawling bush and blooms later
than common azaleas. Its blossoms stand for waves and
the white sand symbolizes the calm sea in Hōrai Garden at
Taichi Temple in Kōga, Shiga prefecture, a rock garden
made by Kobori Enshū (Kobori Masakazu, 1579–1647).

苔青し

　　　京の古刹の

　　　　　息静か

こけあおし

　　　きょうのこさつの

　　　　　いきしずか

季語　苔青し（夏）

苔の美しいことで有名な京都の西方寺は、通称、苔寺とい

われる。

Koke aoshi

> Kyō no kosatsu no

> > iki shizuka

The green moss is quietly breathing

> at the old temple

> > in the ancient capital

Season word: *koke aoshi* (the moss is green; summer)

Saihō Temple in Kyoto is generally known as *Koke dera* (Moss Temple).

夏の月

　　真珠のやうに

　　　　浮かびたり

なつのつき

　　しんじゅのように

　　　　うかびたり

季語　夏の月（夏）

真珠は、ムーンストーンとともに6月の誕生石である。6月1日は、「真珠の日」。一方、7月11日は、真珠王、御木本幸吉（1858年–1954年）が、1893年に真珠養殖に成功した日で、「真珠記念日」として指定されている。

Natsu no tsuki

    shinju no yōni

        ukabi tari

The summer moon

    is floating in the sky

        like a pearl

Season word: *natsu no tsuki* (summer moon; summer)

Pearl is the birthstone for June, along with moonstone.

June 1 is the Day of Pearls, while July 11 is designated as

the Day to Celebrate Pearls. On July 11, 1893, Mikimono

Kōkichi (1858–1954), the Pearl King of Japan, succeeded

in cultivating pearls for the first time.

夏の空

　　竜宮に飛ぶ

　　　「はやぶさ2」

なつのそら

　　りゅうぐうにとぶ

　　　はやぶさ2

季語　　夏の空（夏）

2014年12月に鹿児島県の種子島宇宙センターから打ち上げられた小惑星探査機「はやぶさ2」が目的地である小惑星リュウグウに2018年6月21日からに7月5日の間に到着予定であると発表された。そして6月27日に到着した。

Natsu no sora

Ryūgū ni tobu

Hayabusa 2

In the summer sky

Hayabusa 2 is flying

to the asteroid Ryūgū

Season word: *natsu no sora* (summer sky; summer)

The asteroid sample-return mission Hayabusa 2 (Peregrine falcon 2) that had been launched from the Tanegashima Space Center in December 2014 arrived at its target, the near-Earth asteroid 162173 Ryūgū, on June 27, 2018.

July

Photograph 7. Sea of clouds at Takeda Castle, under Wikimedia Commons license, "Takeda Castle," December 5, 2010, https://commons.wikimedia.org/wiki/File:Flickr_-_bullets95_-_DSC01859.jpg

短夜や

　　星の学校

　　　　夏休み

みじかよや

　　ほしのがっこう

　　　　なつやすみ

季語　短夜（夏）　夏休み（夏）

Mijika yo ya

   hoshi no gakkō

      natsu yasumi

During the short nights in summer

   the star school

      is in recess

Season words: *mijika yo* (a short night in summer;

summer) and *natsu yasumi* (summer recess; summer)

旱星大接近

　　西郷どんと

　　　再会す

ひでりぼしだいせっきん

　　さいごうどんと

　　　さいかいす

季語　旱星（火星やアンタレスなどの赤い星、夏）

旱星は、炎天続きの旱を象徴するような、夏に見える赤い星の

こと。2018年7月31日、火星が15年振りに地球に大接近（6千

万キロ弱）した。火星は、西南戦争のあった1877年にも大接近

し、当時は、西郷隆盛（1828年—1877年）にちなんで「西郷星」

と呼ばれた。南洲翁は、鹿児島の南洲神社に祀られている。次

の同規模の火星大接近は、2035年になるという。

Hideri boshi dai sekkin

Saigō don to

saikai su

Mars approaching the closest to Earth

meets General Saigō again

after 141 years

Season word: *hideri boshi* (red star and planet observed in

the heat of summer, such as Antares and Mars; summer)

Mars approached the closest to Earth in July 2018. The last time

this happened was in 1877 when Saigō Takamori (1828–1877)

was defeated in the Satsuma Rebellion, in Kagoshima. Mars in

1877 was called the "Saigō Star" as a tribute to the general, who

was one of the founding fathers of the Meiji government and the

last samurai. He is enshrined in Nanshū Shrine in Kagoshima.

雲海や

　　浮かぶ城址

　　　　秘めし恋

うんかいや

　　うかぶしろあと

　　　　ひめしこい

季語　雲海（夏）

兵庫県朝来（あさご）市にある竹田城跡は、壮大な雲海で
知られ、「天空の城」と呼ばれる。

Unkai ya

ukabu shiro ato

himehi koi

In the sea of clouds

float the ruins of the castle

that has a secret love story to tell

Season word: *unkai* (sea of clouds; summer)

The ruins of Takeda Castle in Asago, Hyōgo prefecture, are known for a magical and spectacular view of the vast stone foundations covered by mist at dawn and are called "Castle in the Sky."

日照り雲

　　ターナーの光

　　　　たなびきて

ひでりぐも

　　ターナーのひかり

　　　　たなびきて

季語　　日照り雲（夏）

日照り雲は、夏の日没の頃に紅色に染まった巴（ともえ）

形の雲のこと。J. M. W. ターナー（1775年−1851年）は、

雄大な空の雲と光を巧妙に描いた英国の風景画家。

Hideri gumo

Tānā no hikari

tanabiki te

The swirling clouds in the summer evening

are shining

with the light of Turner

Season word: *hideri gumo* (swirling clouds in the summer

evening; summer)

Turner refers to the English painter, J. M. W. Turner

(1775–1851), who drew spectacular landscapes and skies.

梅花の藻

　　川の揺りかご

　　　　游びたり

ばいかのも

　　かわのゆりかご

　　　　あそびたり

季語　梅花の藻（梅花藻、夏）

梅花藻（バイカモ）は、清流に棲息し初夏に白い小花を咲かせる渓流植物。滋賀県米原市、琵琶湖北部を流れる地蔵川や福島県郡山市の清水川などがバイカモの生育地には、開花時に多くの観光客が訪れる。

Baika no mo

    kawa no yurikago

      asobi tari

The water buttercups

    are playing with the cradle

      of the clear running water

Season word: *baika no mo* (*baika mo, lit.,* "plum blossom aquaplant," water buttercup; summer)

This aquaplant has white flowers that look like plum blossoms, hence the name. They only grow in clean running water, such as the Jizō River in Maibara, Shiga prefecture (in northern Lake Biwa) and the Shimizu River in Kōriyama, Fukushima prefecture.

追良瀬川

　　　鮎の上りて

　　　　　風香る

おいらせがわ

　　　あゆののぼりて

　　　　　かぜかおる

季語　　鮎（夏）

追良瀬川は、青森県西津軽郡を流れ、日本海に注ぐ。その渓谷は、鮎釣りで有名。天然アユは香魚と言われるほど清々しい香りがする。養殖鮎にはない香りであるという。

Oirase gawa

ayu no nobori te

kaze kaoru

In the Oirase River

the sweetfish runs up the stream

and the wind carries its sweet scent

Season word: *ayu* (sweetfish; summer)

The valley of the Oirase River in Nishi–Tsugaru, Aomori

prefecture, is known for sweetfish fishing. It is said that

the natural sweetfish has a refreshing sweet aroma, whereas

the farmed one does not.

夏の空

　　無人の島の

　　　　「鳥の歌」

なつのそら

　　むじんのしまの

　　　　とりのうた

季語　　夏の空（夏）

「鳥の歌」は、世界的チェロ奏者パブロ・カザルス（1876年

－1973年）が、世界平和を訴えて演奏したカタルーニャ民

謡。2018年夏、九州、天草諸島の孤島にある、潜伏キリ

シタンゆかりの教会の平和祈念コンサートで演奏された。

Natsu no sora

   mujin no shima no

     "Tori no uta"

Under the summer sky

   the isolated island is listening

     to the "Song of the Birds"

Season word: *natsu no sora* (summer sky; summer)

A concert for peace was held at a church on the abandoned

island of the Amakusa Islands, where the 'hidden Christians'

used to live. It played the Song of the Birds, the traditional

Catalan Christmas song, "El cant dels ocells." The self-exiled

cellist Pablo Casals (1876–1973) played the instrumental

version, making it world famous. He stated that birds in

Catalonia sing "peace, peace."

シーグラス

　　潮風の唄に

　　　　煌きて

シーグラス

　　しおかぜのうたに

　　　　きらめきて

季語　シーグラス（ビーチグラス、夏）

Shii gurasu

shio kaze no uta ni

kirameki te

The sea glass

is glittering

in the song of the sea breeze

Season word: *shii gurasu* (sea glass, beach glass; summer)

炎帝や

　　波照間の

　　　　「最南端の碑」焦がす

えんていや

　　はてるまの

　　　　さいなんたんのひこががす

季語　炎帝（夏）

沖縄県の波照間島は、日本最南端の有人島で、「日本最
南端之碑」が建立されている。

Eitei ya

Hateruma no

"Sai nantan no hi" kogasu

The summer sun god

burns the "Monument for the southernmost point of Japan"

on Hateruma Island

Season word: *entei* (the summer sun god; summer)

Hateruma Island, one of the Yaeyama Islands, in Okinawa

prefecture, is the southernmost inhabited island of Japan.

波照間の夏

　　南十字の

　　　　星仰ぐ

はてるまのなつ

　　みなみじゅうじの

　　　　ほしあおぐ

季語　　夏（夏）

沖縄県の波照間島は、日本最南端の有人島で、日本国内で南十字星を見ることができる数少ない南の島である。

Hateruma no natsu

Minami jūji no

hoshi aogu

In the summer on Hateruma Island

one is gazing

upon the Southern Cross

Season word: *natsu* (summer; summer)

Hateruma Island in Okinawa prefecture is one of the few

islands in Japan where the Southern Cross can be observed.

August

Photograph 8. Mt. Yari, under Wikimedia Commons license, "Mt. Yari from the ridge," August 15, 2013, https://commons.wikimedia.org/wiki/File:北穂東稜から見た槍ヶ岳_2013-08-15_-_Monto_Jari_de_la_monteĝo_-_Mt._Yari_from_the_rigde_-_panoramio.jpg

旱天や

　　農夫の歎き

　　　　詩人泣く

かんてんや

　　のうふのなげき

　　　　しじんなく

季語　旱天（夏）

旱天は、異常な日照り続きの空のこと。宮沢賢治（1896年
−1933年）の詩、「雨ニモマケズ」に寄せて。

Kanten ya

　　nōfu no nageki

　　　shijin naku

In the sky of the severe drought

　　the farmers lamented

　　　and the poet cried

Season word: *kanten* (sky during severe drought; summer)

This is a homage to the compassionate poem, *Ame nimo makezu* (*lit.*, "Undeterred by the Rain," or "Strong in the Rain") by Miyazawa Kenji (1896–1933).

郭公や

　　　歌のレッスン

　　　　　森の聴く

かっこうや

　　　うたのレッスン

　　　　　もりのきく

季語　郭公（カッコウ、夏）

郭公（カッコウ）は、渡り鳥で、初夏に日本に飛来する夏鳥。

宮沢賢治（1896年−1933年）の童話、『セロ弾きのゴーシ

ュ』（1934年）より連想。

Kakkō ya

uta no ressun

mori no kiku

The cuckoo

is having a voice lesson

and the wood is listening

Season word: *kakkō* (common cuckoo; summer)

This an image after the story *Sero-hiki no Gōshu* (Gauche, The Cellist) by Miyazawa Kenji (1896–1933), which was published posthumously in 1934.

夏の宵

　　セロと合奏

　　　狸の子

なつのよい

　　セロとがっそう

　　　たぬきのこ

季語　夏の宵（夏）

宮沢賢治の童話、『セロ弾きのゴーシュ』（1934年）の一
場面。狸は、冬の季語であるが、狸の子は季語ではない。

Natsu no yoi

   sero to gassō

    tanuki no ko

In the summer evening

   the raccoon dog puppy

    is playing music along with the cello

Season word: *natsu no yoi* (summer evening; summer)

This describes a scene in the story *Sero-hiki no Gōshu*

(Gauche, The Cellist, 1934) by Miyazawa Kenji.

御来迎

　　御嶽の小屋

　　　　また拝み

ごらいごう

　　おんたけのこや

　　　　またおがみ

季語　　御来迎（ごらいごう、夏）

御来迎は富士山や木曽の御嶽山などの霊山の山頂で拝

む日の出のこと。2014年年9月の噴火で58人が死亡、5

人が行方不明となった御嶽山では閉鎖されていた二の池

山小屋が「二の池ヒュッテ」として2018年8月に再開した。

Go raigō

    Ontake no koya

        mata ogami

Sunrise on Mt. Ontake

    the mountain hut

        is making prayers again to the mountain

Season word: *go raigō* (the sunrise on sacred mountains to

which people make prayers; summer)

Mt. Ontake, spanning Gifu and Nagano prefectures, erupted

in September 2014, killing 58 people near the summit, with

5 people missing. The mountain lodge reopened in August

2018, after four years of restoration work.

夏深し

　　風を分けたり

　　　　檜穂高

なつふかし

　　かぜをわけたり

　　　　やりほたか

季語　夏深し（夏）

北アルプスの奥穂高岳は、日本で三番目に高い山、槍ヶ
岳は、五番目に高い山である。

Natsu fukashi

kaze o wake tari

Yari Hotaka

In the late summer

Mt. Hotaka and Mt. Yari

are splitting the wind

Season word: *natsu fukashi* (late summer; summer)

Mt. Hotaka and Mt. Yari in the Northern Japan Alps are the third and fifth highest mountains in Japan and are popular destinations for mountaineering in the summer.

雲の峰

　　桴の音響く

　　　津軽富士

くものみね

　　ばちのねひびく

　　　つがるふじ

季語　.雲の峰（入道雲、夏）

桴（ばち）は、津軽じょんがら節を伴奏する三味線の桴のこと。

Kumo no mine

bachi no ne hibiku

Tsugaru Fuji

The cumulonimbus clouds

the sound of the shamisen pick

reverberates on Mt. Tsugaru–Fuji

Season word: *kumo no mine* (cumulonimbus clouds;

summer)

Mt. Iwaki in Hirosaki, Aomori prefecture, is called Mt.

Tsugaru–Fuji for its graceful shape like that of Mt. Fuji.

The Tsugaru region is famous for its traditional songs,

accompanies by the shamisen string instrument.

灼くる海

　　　沖縄の色

　　　　　蘇り

やくるうみ

　　　おきなわのいろ

　　　　　よみがえり

季語　灼く（夏）

1945年3月−6月の沖縄戦で失われた沖縄の原風景を、

AIが白黒写真に色を付けることによって復元した。鮮や

かな色によって、地元民の記憶が呼び起される。

Yakuru umi

Okinawa no iro

yomigaeri

The burning hot summer sea

has revived

the colors of Okinawa

Season word: *yaku* (burning hot in summer; summer)

The original landscapes and the ways of the local people of

Okinawa before World War II that had been lost in the war

were restored by the AI coloration of black-and-white

photographs that were found.

夏時雨

　　グスコーブドリ

　　　偲びたり

なつしぐれ

　　グスコーブドリ

　　　しのびたり

季語　夏時雨（夏にしとしとと静かに降る雨、夏）

宮沢賢治の『グスコーブドリの伝記』（1932年）に寄せて。

Natsu shigure

Gusukō Budori

shinobi tari

The summer drizzle

is reminiscing about

Gusukō Budori

Season word: *natsu shigure* (summer drizzle; summer)

This is after *Gusukō Budori no denki* (Life of Gusukō

Budori, 1932) by Miyazawa Kenji, in which the protagonist

Gusukō Budori sacrifices himself by going to the volcano

and blasting it, in order to release CO_2 to warm up the

famine-stricken community in the cold weather.

黄泉国

　　よだかの願ひ

　　　叶へたり

よもつくに

　　よだかのねがい

　　　かなえたり

季語　よだか（夜鷹、一般的には「よたか」と読む、夏）
宮沢賢治の名作、『よだかの星』(1934年)へのオマージ
ュ。賢治は天文学にも通じていて、1572年にカシオペア
座の中に発見された、SN 1572「ティコ（チコ）の超新星」
を心に描いて『よだかの星』を書いたと考えられている。

Yomotsu kuni

yodaka no negai

kanae tari

The gods of the land of death

have granted the dying wish

of the nighthawk

Season word: *yodaka* (or "*yotada*," nighthawk; summer)

The nighthawk, or grey nightjar, refers to the protagonist in the

story, *Yodaka no hoshi* (The Nighthawk Star) by Miyazawa

Kenji (1896–1933), in which the ugly nocturnal bird had been

bullied by other birds and wished to die in the sky. In the end,

he became a magnificent star. It is considered that Miyazawa

had in mind the "Nighthawk Star" to be SN 1527, or Tycho's

Supernova, discovered in the constellation Cassiopeia in 1572.

七夕や

　　銀河鉄道

　　　　臨時便

たなばたや

　　ぎんがてつどう

　　　　りんじびん

季語　七夕（旧暦の7月7日、秋）

俳句の歳時記は、旧暦（太陰暦）を採用しているので、七夕の7月7日は秋となる。宮沢賢治（1896年−1933年）の『銀河鉄道の夜』（1934年）より連想。

Tanabata ya

Ginga tetsudō

rinji bin

On the night of the Star Festival

one gets on the special train

of the Milky Way Railroad

Season word: *Tanabata* (Star Festival, July 7 in the lunar calendar, which falls in autumn; autumn)

In haiku, autumn begins on August 7. This is inspired by Miyazawa Kenji's posthumously published story *Ginga testudō no yoru* (The Night of the Milky Way Railroad).

September

Photograph 9. Porcelain art pair created by Meg Itoh after the nursery rhyme, Hey Diddle Diddle, the Cow Jumped over the Moon, taken by the author

又三郎

　　二百十日の

　　　　風となり

またさぶろう

　　にひゃくとおかの

　　　　かぜとなり

季語　　二百十日（秋）

宮沢賢治（1896年−1933年）の作品、『風の又三郎』より

連想。賢治の死後、1934年に出版された。

Matasaburō

   Nihyaku tōka no

      kaze to nari

Matasaburō the Wind

   came to the village

      on the Two Hundred and Tenth Day

Season word: *Nihyaku tōka* (the two hundred and tenth day from the day of the arrival of spring [February 4], which usually falls on September 1, except in a leap year; autumn)

Matasaburō refers to the protagonist in *Kaze no Matasaburō* (Matasaburō the Wind, 1934) by Miyazawa Kenji, whom the villagers think to be the legendary son of the spirit of the wind. The Two Hundred and Tenth Day is the day of warning for Japanese farmers of the arrival of the typhoon season.

秋暁や

　　「はやぶさ2」

　　　竜宮着陸す

しゅうぎょうや

　　はやぶさ2

　　　りゅうぐうちゃくりくす

季語　　秋暁（しゅうぎょう、秋の夜明け、秋）

2014年12月に打ち上げられた小惑星探査機はやぶさ2

が、2018年9月目的地のリュウグウ（地球と火星の軌道付

近を回る）着陸に成功、地表探査を開始した。2019年12

月にリュウグウを出発、2020年12月に地球に戻る予定。

Shūgyō ya

    Hayabusa 2

        Ryūgū chakuriku su

At the autumn dawn

    Hayabusa 2

        landed on the asteroid Ryūgū

Season word: *shūgyō* (autumn dawn; autumn)

In September 2018, Hayabusa 2 (Peregrine falcon 2), the asteroid sample-return mission that was launched from the Tanegashima Space Center in December 2014, landed on its target, the near-Earth asteroid 162173 Ryūgū, and began exploration of the surface. It is to depart the asteroid in December 2019 and return to Earth in December 2020.

秋麗

　　ゆつくり欠ける

　　　　白き月

あきうらら

　　ゆつくりかける

　　　　しろきつき

季語　　秋麗（あきうらら、秋のよく晴れた日、秋）

Aki urara

yukkuri kakeru

shiroki tsuki

On the fine autumn day

the white moon is waning

slowly

Season word: *aki urara* (fine autumn day; autumn)

On September 4, 2018, a beautiful waning moon was

observed in broad daylight.

名月や

　　天の遣はし

　　　　竹の姫

めいげつや

　　てんのつかわし

　　　　たけのひめ

季語　名月（秋）

『源氏物語』にも言及されている『竹取物語』に寄せて。

Meigetsu ya

    ten no tsukawashi

        take no hime

On the night of the autumn full moon

    the lord of heaven has sent

        the princess into the bamboo

Season word: *mei getsu* (fine full moon of mid-autumn; autumn)

This is an image after the Japanese folklore story, *Taketori monogatari* (The Tale of the Bamboo Cutter), in which an old man finds a little girl in a bamboo shoot, who had been sent from heaven.

天満月

　　時の巡りて

　　　　姫の逝く

あまみつき

　　ときのめぐりて

　　　　ひめのゆく

季語　天満月（あまみつき、秋）

『竹取物語』の一場面より。

Ama mitsuki

   toki no meguri te

      hime no yuku

On the night of the autumn full moon

   after many years

      the princess is going back

Season word: *ama mitsuki* (full moon of autumn; autumn)

This refers to a scene in *Taketori monogatari* (The Tale of the Bamboo Cutter), where Princess Kaguya is ascending to heaven.

ヴァイオリン

　　二色の秋

　　　　奏でたり

ヴァイオリン

　　ふたいろのあき

　　　　かなでたり

季語　秋（秋）

宮沢賢治の『セロ弾きのゴーシュ』より連想。

Vaiorin

    futa iro no aki

        kanade tari

The violin

    is playing

        the two colors of autumn

Season word: *aki* (autumn; autumn)

This is an image after the story *Sero-hiki no Gōshu* (Gauche, The Cellist, 1934) by Miyazawa Kenji (1896–1933).

流れ星

　　賢治の阿修羅

　　　　流れゆく

ながれぼし

　　けんじのあしゅら

　　　　ながれゆく

季語　　流れ星(秋)

口語詩『心象スケッチ　春と修羅』(1924年)を著した宮沢賢治。修羅(阿修羅)は賢治の煩悩と解釈することができる。

Nagare boshi

Kenji no Ashura

nagare yuku

The shooting star

is making the Asura in Kenji

drift away

Season word: *nagare boshi* (shooting star; autumn)

Miyazawa Kenji (1896–1933) wrote an anthology of poems

entitled *Haru to Shura* (An Asura in Spring). Asura,

power-seeking deities, or the gods of anger, with three

heads and three faces and six arms in Hinduism, became

deities symbolizing belligerence in Buddhism. Asura could

be interpreted as a demon in Kenji.

カシオペア

　　「星めぐりの歌」

　　　口遊み

カシオペア

　　ほしめぐりのうた

　　　くちずさみ

季語　カシオペア（カシオペア座、秋）

「星めぐりの歌」は、宮沢賢治（1896年－1933年）の作

詞・作曲。ユーチューブで聞くことができる。リンクは、

https://www.youtube.com/watch?v=HHNEhT2Ckck

Kashiopea

    "Hoshi meguri no uta"

        kuchi zusami

Cassiopeia

    is humming

        the tune of the "Song of the Star-Circling Tour"

Season word: *Kashiopea* (constellation Cassiopeia;

autumn)

Miyazawa Kenji wrote the lyrics and composed the music

for *Hoshi meguri no uta* (Song of the Star-Circling Tour):

https://www.youtube.com/watch?v=HHNEhT2Ckck.

星月夜

　　銀河鉄道

　　　永遠の旅立ち

ほしづきよ

　　ぎんがてつどう

　　　とわのたびだち

季語　星月夜（月のように輝く星の美しい夜空、秋）

9月21日は、宮沢賢治（1896年−1933年）の命日。賢治の『銀河鉄道の夜』（1934年）に寄せて。

Hoshi zuki yo

  Ginga tetsudō

    towa no tabi dachi

In the starlit autumn night

  the Milky Way Railway

    departs for the trip to eternity

Season word: *hoshi zuki yo* (starlit autumn night as bright

as the moonlight; autumn)

This is a memorial tribute to Miyazawa Kenji (1896–1933),

who died on September 21, inspired by his *Ginga testudō*

no yoru (The Night of the Milky Way Railroad, 1934).

「賢治の忌」

　　星河奏でる

　　　　セロの音や

けんじのき

　　せいがかなでる

　　　　セロのねや

季語　「賢治の忌」（9月21日、秋）　星河（天の川、秋）

9月21日は、宮沢賢治（1896年−1933年）の命日。賢治の『セロ弾きのゴーシュ』（1934年）に寄せて。

Kenji no ki

   seiga kanaderu

      sero no ne ya

On the memorial day of Kenji

   the Milky Way

      is playing the cello

Season words: *Kenji-ki* (anniversary memorial day of

Miyazawa Kenji's death, September 21; autumn) and *seiga*

(Milky Way; autumn)

This memorial tribute of Miyazawa Kenji is inspired by his

story *Sero-hiki no Gōshu* (Gauche, The Cellist, 1934).

October

Photograph 10. Hanging persimmons, under Wikimedia Commons license, "Barn of Kanzo yashiki," November 12, 2010, https://upload.wikimedia.org/wikipedia/commons/7/72/Kanzo-yashiki-umaya.JPG

草紅葉

　　野山を遊ぶ

　　　　賢治とトシ

くさもみじ

　　のやまをあそぶ

　　　　けんじとトシ

季語　　草紅葉（秋）

宮沢賢治の妹トシ（1898年−1922年）は、賢治の最大の理解者であった。日本女子大学卒業後、母校の花巻高等女学校の教師となるが、結核を患い、24歳の若さで亡くなる。

Kusa momiji

noyama o asobu

Kenji to Toshi

The autumn coloration of the grass

the mountain field finds

Kenji and Toshi playing among the colors

Season word: *kusa momiji* (autumn coloration of the grass; autumn)

Miyazawa Kenji's younger sister Toshi (1898–1922) was the most ardent supporter of his works. She graduated from the Japan Women's University and began teaching at her alma mater, the Hanamaki Higher Women's School, but then died of tuberculosis at age 24.

榧の森

　　どんぐりと

　　　　猫の裁判長

かやのもり

　　どんぐりと

　　　　ねこのさいばんちょう

季語　どんぐり（団栗、秋）

宮沢賢治が生前に唯一出版した作品集、『注文の多い料
理店』（1924年）に収録された短編、『どんぐりと山猫』に
寄せて。

Kaya no mori

    donguri to

        neko no saibanchō

The woods of the Japanese nutmeg-yew

    watch the trial of acorns

        with the cat as the judge

Season word: *donguri* (acorns; autumn)

This refers to a curious story *Donguri to yama neko* (The Acorns and the Mountain Cat, 1924) by Miyazawa Kenji, in which a mountain cat plays the judge for a trial of acorns.

嵐山

　　秋風を連れ

　　　　逍遥す

あらしやま

　　あきかぜをつれ

　　　　しょうようす

季語　秋風(秋)

Arashiyama

    aki kaze o tsure

        shōyō su

In Arashiyama

    one is strolling

        accompanied by the autumn wind

Season word: *aki kaze* (autumn wind; autumn)

Arashiyama is one of the most popular tourist destinations

in Kyoto.

露と寝る

　　野宿の一夜

　　　　「露伴」生む

つゆとねる

　　のじゅくのひとよ

　　　　ろはんうむ

季語　　露（秋）

幸田露伴（1867年−1947年）は、電信技師として北海道

余市に赴任するが、ほどなく職を放棄し、帰京した。帰途、

ほぼ無一文となり、汽車賃を節約するため福島から徒歩。

二本松で野宿した時、「里遠しいざ露と寝ん草枕」と詠ん

だ。この体験が、「露伴」というペンネームの由来という。

Tsuyu to neru

nojuku no hitoyo

"Rohan" umu

Sleeping with dewdrops outdoors

in the night

gave birth to the penname Rohan

Season word: *tsuyu* (dewdrops; autumn)

The writer Kōda Rohan (1867–1947) based his penname on an

experience in his youth when he quit his job as a telegraph

engineer in Yoichi, Hokkaidō, and travelled back to Tokyo

almost penniless. He slept in a field covered with dewdrops in

Nihonmatsu, Fukuoka prefecture, which inspired him to take

Rohan (*lit.*, to accompany dewdrops) as his penname.

八幡宮

　　大銀杏の

　　　　秋再び

はちまんぐう

　　おおいちょうの

　　　　あきふたたび

季語　　秋（秋）

銀杏の木は季語でない。銀杏（ぎんなん）は、秋の季語。

鎌倉八幡宮の大銀杏は、2010年3月10日未明、雪嵐で

倒れたが、まもなく再生の取り組みが施された。翌年、若

芽が移植されて蘇生し、2013年には黄色く色づいた。

Hachiman gū

ō ichō no

aki futatabi

At Hachiman Shrine

the giant ginko tree

greets the autumn again

Season word: *aki* (autumn; autumn)

Hachiman Shrine in Kamakura, Kanagawa prefecture, had

a famous giant ginko tree. In March 2010, it fell during a

snowstorm and a resuscitation project started immediately.

Transplanted saplings from the old tree were successful and

their leaves turned yellow in autumn.

秋時雨

　　木曽路は全て

　　　　雨の中

あきしぐれ

　　きそじはすべて

　　　　あめのなか

季語　秋時雨（秋）

島崎藤村（1872年−1943年）の長編小説、『夜明け前』
の冒頭句、「木曽路はすべて山の中である。」より連想。

Aki shigure

    Kisoji wa subete

        ame no naka

In the autumn drizzle

    the Kiso Road

        is all under the rain

Season word: *aki shigure* (autumn drizzle; autumn)

This is taken from the novel, *Yoake mae* (Before the Dawn) by Shimazaki Tōson (1872–1943), which begins with "The Kiso Road is all in the mountains."

山霧や

　　馬籠の宿の

　　　　夜明け前

やまぎりや

　　まごめのやどの

　　　　よあけまえ

季語　霧（秋）

岐阜県中津川市にある馬籠は、『夜明け前』の作者、島崎藤村（1872年−1943年）の生誕地である。信州・木曽を通る中山道の宿場町として栄えた。

Yama giri ya

    Magome no yado no

        yoake mae

The mist in the mountains

    covers the inn in Magome

        before the dawn

Season word: *kiri* (mist; autumn)

The writer Shimazaki Tōson was born in Magome in current Nakatsugawa, Gifu prefecture. Magome was a station on the Nakasendō Road that ran through Kiso and Shinshū, and the local inns prospered.

中山道

　　　七竈の実の

　　　　　道案内

なかせんどう

　　　ななかまどのみの

　　　　　みちあない

季語　七竈の実（秋）

七竈（ななかまど）は、その赤い実が、七度かまどに入れて
も、燃え残るほど燃えにくいことから命名されたという。

Nakasendō

   nana kamado no mi no

      michi anai

On the Nakasendō Road

   the berries of the Japanese rowan

      guide the traveler

Season word: *nana kamado no mi* (berries of the Japanese rowan; autumn)

The Japanese rowan bears bright red berries in autumn.

飛騨の里

　　　渋柿吊るす

　　　　　空澄みし

ひだのさと

　　　しぶがきつるす

　　　　　そらすみし

季語　渋柿（柿、秋）

岐阜県の飛騨地方は、柿の産地として有名。南飛騨富士
柿などのブランド品がある。

Hida no sato

    shibu gaki tsurusu

        sora sumishi

In the fields of Hida

    the bitter persimmons are hung

        under the clear blue sky

Season word: *shibu gaki* (*kaki*, persimmon; autumn)

Hida is a mountainous northern region of Gifu prefecture.
Japanese dry bitter persimmons by hanging them under the
house eaves until they lose tannin and become sweet.

天の川

　　アンドロメダの

　　　身を案ず

あまのがわ

　　アンドロメダの

　　　みをあんず

季語　天の川（秋）　アンドロメダ（アンドロメダ座、秋）

ギリシア神話によると、古代エチオピアの王ケフェウスと女

王カシオペアの娘アンドロメダは、ゼウスとポセイドンの怒

りを鎮めるため、生贄として岩にくくりつけられ、海の怪物

ケートュスに与えられたが、英雄ペルセウスに救出された。

Ama no gawa

Andoromeda no

mi o anzu

The Milky Way

is concerned for the plight of

Princess Andromeda

Season words: *Ama no gawa* (Milky Way; autumn) and *Andoromeda* (constellation Andromeda; autumn) In Greek mythology, Andromeda was a daughter of the Aethiopian king Cepheus and queen Cassiopeia. In order to quell the wrath of Zeus and of Poseidon, Andromeda was offered to the sea monster Cetus and was stripped and chained to a rock, until Perseus rescued her.

November

Photograph 11. Dwarf periwinkle after the sleet, taken by

the author

冬紅葉

　　「吾はわれ也」

　　　哲学の道

ふゆもみじ

　　われはわれなり

　　　てつがくのみち

季語　　冬紅葉（冬）

京都の哲学の道は、『善の研究』で知られる哲学者、西田
幾多郎（1870年－1945年）が琵琶湖疏水支流沿いの小
道を散策し、思想に耽ったことからこう名付けられた。道の
途中には、西田幾多郎の「人は人、吾はわれ也、とにかく
吾行く道を吾は行くなり」と刻まれた石碑がある。

Fuyu momiji

ware wa ware nari

Tetsugaku no michi

The maple foliage in winter

the philosopher is going his way

on the Philosopher's Walk

Season word: *fuyu momiji* (maple foliage in winter; winter)

One of the most popular tourist destinations in Kyoto, the

Philosopher's Walk along the canal between Ginkaku

Temple and Nanzen Temple is named after the philosopher

Nishida Kitaro (1870–1945), who used to stroll the path

and philosophize. The stone with his poem stands there.

霜の降る

　　イーハトーブの

　　　　森遥か

しものふる

　　イーハトーブの

　　　　もりはるか

季語　霜降る（冬）

「イーハトーブ」は、宮沢賢治の作品に登場する岩手県地方の風土を理想化した架空の地名。2005年、これに該当する六ヶ所の風景地が、「イーハトーブの風景地」として、国の名勝に指定された。

Shimo no furu

Iihatōbu no

mori haruka

The frost is falling

the woods of Ihatov

loom far away

Season word: *shimo furu* (frost falls; winter)

Ihatov, arguably derived from Iwate, is a toponym created

by Miyazawa Kenji, modelled after landscapes of his

birthplace, Iwate prefecture. They inspired him to write

many of his stories. In 2005, six actual places that matched

the landscapes of Ihatov were collectively designated as a

Place of Scenic Beauty of Japan.

散紅葉

　　パウダーシュガーの

　　雪の朝

ちりもみじ

　　パウダーシュガーの

　　ゆきのあさ

季語　散紅葉（冬）　雪（冬）

散り敷いた紅葉に降った雪の白のコントラスが美しい。

Chiri momiji

   paudā sugā no

      yuki no asa

The fallen maple leaves

   are covered by the powdered-sugar-like snow

      in the morning

Season words: *chiri momiji* (fallen maple leaves; winter)

and *yuki* (snow; winter)

霜の花

　　下総の野を

　　　　埋め尽くし

しものはな

　　しもおさののを

　　　　うめつくし

季語　霜の花（冬）

霜の花は、霜の雅語。下総（しもおさ）は、現在の千葉県

北部と茨城県西部に相当する藩。

Shimo no hana

Shimōsa no no o

ume tsukushi

The frost flowers

have spread over

the fields of Shimōsa

Season word: *shimo no hana* (*lit.*, "frost flowers"; winter)

Shimo no hana is a poetic name for frost. Shimōsa was a

province (state) that corresponds to current northern Chiba

prefecture and western Ibaraki prefecture.

道後の温泉

　　ロシアの捕虜よ

　　　　冬の空

どうごのゆ

　　ロシアのほりよよ

　　　　ふゆのそら

季語　　冬の空（冬）

愛媛県松山市には日露戦争（1904年−1905年）中、露人俘虜収

容所があり、地元住民が手厚く待遇した。将校は広い邸宅に住み

外出も自由で道後温泉や観劇をし、下級兵士は寺の宿坊に住み

海水浴や観光旅行へ行った。第二次大戦後日本人捕虜が極寒の

シベリアで強制労働に従事させられたのとは雲泥の差であった。

Dōgo no yu

Roshia no horyo yo

fuyu no sora

The Dōgo hot spring

consoled the Russian prisoners of war

under the winter sky

Season word: *fuyu no sora* (winter sky; winter)

Dōgo hot spring in Matsuyama, Ehime prefecture, is one of

the three oldest hot springs in Japan. During the Russo-

Japanese War (1904–1905), the Russian POWs in

Matsuyama were treated generously, and enjoyed outdoor

activities including taking baths at Dōgo hot spring.

初雪や

　　イーハトーブの

　　　　息白し

はつゆきや

　　イーハトーブの

　　　　いきしろし

季語　初雪（冬）　息白し（冬）

「イーハトーブ」は、宮沢賢治の作品に登場する岩手県地

方の風土を理想化した架空の地名。実在する、2005年に、

鞍掛山、七つ森、狼森、釜淵の滝、五輪峠、種山ケ原の6

カ所が「イーハトーブの風景地」に指定され、その後、イギ

リス海岸が追加指定された。

Hatsu yuki ya

    Iihatōbu no

        iki shiroshi

The first snow of the season

    the fields of Ihatov

        are breathing out white breath

Season words: *hatsu yuki* (first snow of the season; winter)
and *iki shiroshi* (breathing out white breath; winter)
Ihatov, arguably derived from Iwate, is a toponym created
by Miyazawa Kenji, modelled after landscapes of his
birthplace, Iwate prefecture. In 2005, six actual places that
matched the landscapes of Ihatov were collectively
designated as a Place of Scenic Beauty of Japan.

霙降る

　　永訣の朝

　　　　トシの朝

みぞれふる

　　えいけつのあさ

　　　　トシのあさ

季語　　霙（冬）

妹トシを悼む宮沢賢治の詩「永訣の朝」。死の直前、トシは
「アメユジュトテチテケンジャ（雨水を取って来てくれ）」と賢
治に頼む。成績優秀で岩手県立花巻高等女子学校を経
て日本女子大学卒業、母校の教師となるが結核のため死
去。享年24才（1898年11月5日－1922年11月27日）。

Mizore furu

eiketsu no asa

Toshi no asa

It is sleeting

on the morning

of the last farewell to Toshi

Season word: *mizore* (sleet; winter)

This is a homage to Miyazawa Kenji's poem, "Eiketsu no

asa" (The Morning of the Last Farewell), in which he

laments the imminent death of his younger sister Toshi

(November 1898–November 1922). Before her death, she

asked him to bring her a scoop of rain water for her to sip.

She died of tuberculosis on November 27, at age 24.

凩や

　　賢治の慟哭

　　　　吹き消さん

こがらしや

　　けんじのどうこく

　　　　ふきけさん

季語　凩（こがらし、冬）

Kogarashi ya

Kenji no dōkoku

fuki kesan

The strong wintry wind

is blowing hard

as if to blow out Kenji's grief

Season word: *kogarashi* (strong wintry wind, winter)

霜柱

　　踏みしめ越へし

　　　野麦峠

しもばしら

　　ふみしめこえし

　　　のむぎとうげ

季語　霜柱（冬）

山本茂実（1917年−1998年）のノンフィクション、『あゝ野麦峠　ある製糸工女哀史』（1968年）に寄せて。戦前、岐阜県飛騨地方の農家の娘達が、険しい野麦峠を越えて、信州（長野県）の岡谷にある製糸工場（生糸生産）へ働きに出て、過酷な労働に従事した事実を描く。

Shimo bashira

fumi shime koeshi

Nomugi tōge

Stepping on the needle ice

the girls have crossed

Nomugi Pass

Season word: *shimo bashira* (needle ice; winter)

Nomugi Pass is located at the border between Gifu prefecture

and Nagano prefecture. Yamamoto Shigemi (1917–1998) wrote

the nonfiction, *Ā Nomugi-tōge: Aru seishi kōjo aishi* (Ah,

Nomugi Pass: The Sad History of Female Workers at Silk Mills,

1968), in which girls in the Hida region in Gifu prefecture

crossed the steep mountain pass on foot and worked at silk mills

in Okaya, Nagano prefecture, where they were exploited.

風花や

　　淡き想ひを

　　　　撒き散らし

かざはなや

　　あわきおもいを

　　　　まきちらし

季語　風花（かざはな、晴天に散らつく小片の雪、冬）

製糸工場で働いていた若い女工は、乙女心を心の奥にし

まい込んで、厳しい搾取的労働に勤しんだ。

Kaza hana ya

    awaki omoi o

        maki chirashi

The small snowflakes on the fine day

    are scattering away

        the innocent feelings of the girl workers

Season word: *kaza haha* (*lit.*, "wind flower," refers to small snowflakes falling on a fine day; winter)

The young female workers at the silk mills in Nagao prefecture tucked deep in their hearts the innocent feelings of young girls and engaged in the exploitative work.

December

Photograph 12. Shirakawa-gō, under Creative Commons license, "Ogimachi, Shirakawa, Ono District, Gifu Prefecture," December 6, 2014, https://commons.wikimedia.org/wiki/File:Ogimachi,_Shira kawa,_Ono_District,_Gifu_Prefecture_501-5627,_Japan_-_panoramio_(21).jpg

初冠雪

　　穂高の峰の

　　　　畏まる

はつかんせつ

　　ほたかのみねの

　　　　かしこまる

季語　初冠雪（冬）

Hatsu kan setsu

Hotaka no mine no

kashikomaru

The first snowcap formation

the summit of Mt. Hotaka

looks solemn

Season word: *hatsu kansetsu* (first snowcap formation of

the season on a mountain; winter)

Mt. Hotaka is part of the Northern Japan Alps and the

second highest mountain in Japan, after Mt. Fuji.

細雪

　　白き鬣

　　　　木曽路ゆく

ささめゆき

　　しろきたてがみ

　　　　きそじゆく

季語　細雪（冬）

「白き鬣」は、雪を被った木曽馬のこと。本州に唯一残る在

来種の馬で、絶滅危惧種に指定されている。

Sasame yuki

   shiroki tategami

      Kisoji yuku

In the fine, light snow

   the white mane

      is trotting on the Kiso Road

Season word: *sasame yuki* (fine, light snow; winter)

The "white mane" refers to that of the snow-covered Kiso

Horse. It is the sole indigenous horse breed on the main

island of Japan and is listed as an endangered species.

冬夕焼

　　英虞湾の

　　　　海と島燃ゆ

ふゆゆやけ

　　あごわんの

　　　　うみとしまもゆ

季語　　冬夕焼（冬）

三重県の英虞湾は、伊勢志摩国立公園の一部。無数の
島々が浮かび、風光明媚である。

Fuyu yuyake

    Ago wan no

        umi to shima moyu

In the winter sunset glory

    at Ago Bay

        the islands and the sea are burning

Season word: *yufu yuyake* (winter sunset glory; winter)

Ago Bay, located in Shima, Mie prefecture, is part of the scenic Ise–Shima National Park.

札幌の

　　雪測定する

　　　　時計台

さっぽろの

　　ゆきそくていする

　　　　とけいだい

季語　雪（冬）

北海道札幌市の時計台は、観光地として有名であるが、

元は、札幌農学校（北海道大学の前身）の学生のための

道場であった。

Sapporo no

    yuki sokutei suru

        tokei dai

In Sapporo

    the clock tower

        is measuring the snow

Season word: *yuki* (snow; winter)

Sapporo, the capital of Hokkaidō, has a famous historical

Western-style clock tower, popular for sightseeing. The

building was originally the drill hall of Sapporo

Agricultural College (current Hokkaidō University).

大雪山

　　馬橇の

　　　　鈴連なりて

だいせつざん

　　うまぞりの

　　　　すずつらなりて

季語　馬橇（うまぞり、冬）

北海道の大雪山は、大雪山国立公園の一部で、雄大な

景色が広がる。

Daisetsu zan

    uma zori no suzu

        truranari te

On Mt. Daisetsu

    the bells of the horse sleigh

        are set in a row

Season word: *uma zori* (horse sleigh; winter)

Mt. Daisetsu refers to the Daisetsu Volcanic Mountain Group in Hokkaidō, and part of the Mt. Daisetsu National Park, the largest national park in Japan.

雪しまき

　　足跡のなき

　　　　雪女

ゆきしまき

　　あしあとのなき

　　　　ゆきおんな

季語　雪しまき（激しく吹き巻く吹雪、冬）

Yuki shimaki

ashiato no naki

yuki on'na

In the swirling snowstorm

the snow woman

leaves no footsteps

Season word: *yuki shimaki* (swirling snowstorm; winter)

The snow woman is a spirit in Japanese folklore.

大地凍つ

　　マンモス親子

　　　永眠す

だいちいつ

　　マンモスおやこ

　　　えいみんす

季語　凍つ(冬)

Daichi itsu

manmosu oyako

eimin su

The earth has frozen

and covered up

the family of mammoths forever

Season word: *itsu* (it freezes; winter)

昼神郷

　　冬籠する

　　　　神の温泉や

ひるがみごう

　　ふゆごもりする

　　　　かみのゆや

季語　　冬籠（冬）

長野県下伊那郡阿智村にある昼神（ひるがみ）温泉郷で
は、毎年、12月から2月まで神様が冬籠りするために訪れ、
その神様を湯屋守（ゆやもり）様として祀るという伝統を、
今日まで守っている。

Hirugami gō

    fuyu gokori suru

        kami no yu ya

In Hirugami village

    the gods are wintering

        in the hot spring

Season word: *fuyu gomori* (to winter; winter)

Hirugami-gō community in Achi village, Nagano
prefecture, has preserved the tradition that the gods visit the
community from December to February, to winter. During
this time, the gods protect the villagers in return.

白川郷

　　雪に眠りて

　　　　春を待つ

しらかわごう

　　ゆきにねむりて

　　　　はるをまつ

季語　　雪（冬）

岐阜県にある白川郷は、合掌造りの集落で有名。1995年には、「白川郷・五箇山の合掌造り集落」として、ユネスコ世界遺産に登録された。

Shirakawa gō

    yuki ni nemuri te

        haru o matsu

Shirakawa village

    is asleep in the snow

        waiting for the spring

Season word: *yuki* (snow; winter)

Shirakawa-gō, in Gifu prefecture, is known for its special architecture with steep roofs in order to prevent snow from accumulating on the roofs and damaging the house. The area is designated as a UNESCO World Heritage Site.

冬銀河

　　賢治の祈り

　　　　届けんと

ふゆぎんが

　　けんじのいのり

　　　　とどけんと

季語　冬銀河（冬）

宮沢賢治追悼。合掌。

Fuyu ginga

    Kenji no inori

        todoken to

The winter Milky Way

    one is trying to send

        the prayers of Kenji there

Season word: *fuyu ginga* (winter Milky Way; winter)

This is a memorial tribute to Miyazawa Kenji. RIP.

About the author

Mayumi Itoh is a former Professor of Political Science at the University of Nevada, Las Vegas (UNLV). She has also taught at Princeton University and Queens College, City University of New York (CUNY), and has written more than 15 single-authored books, as well as more than 15 articles in professional journals. Her book titles include:

–*Globalization of Japan: Japanese Sakoku Mentality and U.S. Efforts to Open Japan* (1998)

–*The Hatoyama Dynasty: Japanese Political Leadership Through the Generations* (2003)

–*Japanese War Orphans in Manchuria: Forgotten Victims of World War II* (2010)

–*Japanese Wartime Zoo Policy: The Silent Victims of World War II* (2010)

–*The Origin of Ping-Pong Diplomacy: The Forgotten Architect of Sino-U.S. Rapprochement* (2011)

–Pioneers of Sino-Japanese Relations: Liao and Takasaki (2012)

–Hachi: The Truth of the Life and Legend of the Most Famous Dog in Japan (2013)

–The Origins of Contemporary Sino-Japanese Relations: Zhou Enlai and Japan (2016)

–The Making of China's War with Japan: Zhou Enlai and Zhang Xueliang (2016)

–The Making of China's Peace with Japan: What Xi Jinping Should Learn from Zhou Enlai (2017)

–"Hachi-ko" in Siberia: The True Story of Japanese Prisoners of War and a Dog (2017)

–Hachiko: Solving Twenty Mysteries about the Most Famous Dog in Japan (2017)

–Eliza Ruhamah Scidmore and Japan: The Life and Journeys to the Far East of the American Woman Who Brought "Sakura" to Washington, D.C. (2017)

–*Kaneko Misuzu: Life and Poems of A Lonely Princes* (2018)

–*The Japanese Culture of Mourning Whales: Whale Graves and Memorial Monuments in Japan* (2018)

–*Haikus of All Seasons I: The Heavens and the Earth* (2018)

–*Animals and the Fukushima Nuclear Disaster* (2018)

–*Haikus of All Seasons II: Humanity* (2018)

–*Haikus of All Seasons III: Fauna* (2018)

–*Haikus of All Seasons IV: Flora* (2018)